PRINCEWILL LAGANG

The Art of Wealth: Alice Walton's Journey to Building a Billion-Dollar Empire

First published by PRINCEWILL LAGANG 2023

Copyright © 2023 by Princewill Lagang

All rights reserved. No part of this publication may be reproduced, stored or transmitted in any form or by any means, electronic, mechanical, photocopying, recording, scanning, or otherwise without written permission from the publisher. It is illegal to copy this book, post it to a website, or distribute it by any other means without permission.

Princewill Lagang asserts the moral right to be identified as the author of this work.

First edition

This book was professionally typeset on Reedsy.
Find out more at reedsy.com

Contents

1. Introduction - Unveiling the Portrait of Alice Walton ... 1
2. The Genesis of Ambition ... 3
3. Forging the Vision ... 5
4. Breaking Ground: The Birth of Crystal Bridges ... 7
5. The Canvas Unfolds: Navigating Challenges and Cultivating... ... 9
6. Beyond Boundaries: Global Impact and Legacy Building ... 11
7. Navigating Change: Challenges, Reflections, and the... ... 13
8. The Next Horizon: Innovations, Collaborations, and the... ... 15
9. Legacy in Bloom: The Culmination of a Life's Work ... 17
10. Beyond the Horizon: The Enduring Influence of Alice Walton's... ... 19
11. Epilogue: A Lasting Imprint on the Canvas of Wealth and... ... 21
12. The Continuing Tapestry: Nurturing the Seeds of Change ... 23
13. Reflections on a Storied Journey ... 25
14. Summary ... 27

1

Introduction - Unveiling the Portrait of Alice Walton

In the hushed corridors of wealth and philanthropy, where fortunes are amassed and legacies are crafted, one name stands as a beacon of innovation, purpose, and cultural enrichment—Alice Walton. In this narrative, we embark on a journey through the pages of "The Art of Wealth," a chronicle that unveils the intricate tapestry of a woman whose life has been dedicated to the convergence of commerce, culture, and societal impact.

Born into the legacy of Walmart, Alice Walton's story is more than a tale of financial success; it is a narrative of vision, resilience, and a commitment to reshaping the narrative of wealth in the modern era. As the daughter of Sam Walton, the retail visionary who revolutionized the way America shops, Alice inherits not just a name but a legacy that spans generations.

Our exploration begins in the quaint town of Bentonville, Arkansas, where the Walton family laid the foundation for what would become one of the most iconic retail empires in the world. From these modest beginnings, we trace Alice's footsteps through the corridors of academia, across the global landscape, and into the realms of art, culture, and philanthropy.

The journey is not a linear ascent to wealth; it is a dynamic narrative marked by twists, turns, and moments of introspection. The chapters unfold like brushstrokes on a canvas, revealing the contours of Alice's ambitions, the challenges she faced, and the transformative decisions that shaped her trajectory.

Central to our narrative is the creation of Crystal Bridges Museum of American Art, an architectural marvel nestled in the Ozark Mountains. Through the lens of this cultural institution, we explore how Alice's vision extends beyond profit margins, embracing a commitment to cultural enrichment, education, and community development.

As the narrative unfolds, readers witness the global dimensions of Alice Walton's philanthropy, her strategies for navigating change, and the legacy-building aspects that transcend traditional boundaries. The story invites contemplation on the evolving dynamics of wealth, the responsibilities that accompany affluence, and the enduring impact one woman's journey can have on the collective consciousness of society.

Beyond the confines of a conventional biography, "The Art of Wealth" delves into the intricate interplay of commerce and culture, shaping a narrative that goes beyond financial portfolios to explore the transformative potential of wealth when wielded with intention and purpose.

Join us as we embark on a literary odyssey, unveiling the portrait of Alice Walton—a visionary, a philanthropist, and a steward of wealth whose journey leaves an indelible mark on the canvas of history.

2

The Genesis of Ambition

The sun dipped below the horizon, casting a warm golden glow over the vast expanse of the Ozark Mountains. Nestled within this picturesque landscape was a small town that seemed frozen in time, and it was here, in the heart of Arkansas, that the story of Alice Walton's journey to building a billion-dollar empire began.

As the daughter of Walmart's visionary founder, Sam Walton, Alice inherited not just a name but a legacy steeped in the ethos of hard work and entrepreneurial spirit. This chapter delves into the early days of Alice's life, painting a vivid picture of the modest beginnings that laid the foundation for what would become one of the most remarkable tales of wealth creation in modern history.

Born into the Walton family in 1949, Alice experienced the pulse of small-town America. The streets of Bentonville, Arkansas, where the Waltons resided, were lined with mom-and-pop stores, each with its own story echoing the American Dream. Sam Walton, a retail maverick with an insatiable appetite for innovation, opened the first Walmart store in 1962, forever changing the retail landscape.

THE ART OF WEALTH: ALICE WALTON'S JOURNEY TO BUILDING A BILLION-DOLLAR EMPIRE

Alice, the middle child among the four Walton siblings, grew up witnessing the relentless pursuit of excellence that defined her father. Sam's revolutionary concept of providing everyday low prices for consumers ignited a spark within Alice, igniting her own desire to leave an indelible mark on the world of business.

From an early age, Alice was exposed to the inner workings of the retail giant. She spent weekends and summers working in the family store, absorbing the intricacies of the business like a sponge. The dusty aisles of the five-and-dime store were her playground, and the bustling energy of customers navigating the aisles left an imprint on her entrepreneurial spirit.

However, Alice's journey was not without its challenges. The shadow of her father's success cast both inspiration and expectation. As she matured, Alice grappled with the weight of her family name, determined to carve her own path in the world of business. This chapter unravels the internal conflicts and pivotal moments that shaped Alice's ambitions and fueled her relentless pursuit of success.

"The Art of Wealth" sets the stage for a narrative that transcends business acumen, delving into the personal struggles, triumphs, and the unyielding determination that would propel Alice Walton from the quaint town of Bentonville to the summits of financial prowess. As the first chapter unfolds, readers are invited to witness the genesis of ambition that would eventually lead to the creation of a billion-dollar empire.

3

Forging the Vision

In the hushed corridors of privilege and promise, Alice Walton's journey took an unforeseen turn as she ventured beyond the familiar confines of Bentonville. This chapter chronicles the formative years of her adult life, marked by exploration, self-discovery, and the crystallization of a vision that would shape her destiny.

As Alice stepped onto the vibrant campus of the University of Arkansas, she was not merely a Walton but a seeker of knowledge and purpose. The ivory towers of academia provided a canvas for her to paint her aspirations, and the liberal arts education she pursued became the crucible in which her ambitions were refined. Far from the retail aisles of Walmart, Alice immersed herself in the worlds of art, history, and culture, laying the groundwork for what would later become a defining aspect of her legacy.

The 1970s marked a pivotal era of social change and empowerment, and Alice was not immune to its influence. In the aftermath of the feminist movement, she grappled with the societal expectations placed upon women, aspiring to break free from traditional molds. This chapter unveils the internal struggles and external pressures that fueled Alice's determination to forge a path uniquely her own.

Venturing beyond the Ozarks, Alice immersed herself in the diverse tapestry of America. From the bustling streets of New York City to the serene galleries of Europe, she cultivated a worldly perspective that transcended the aisles of Walmart. This global odyssey not only broadened her horizons but also planted the seeds of an idea—an idea that merged commerce with culture, business with beauty.

The marriage of art and commerce became a central theme in Alice's evolving vision. Her experiences in the art world sparked a passion that went beyond the bottom line, and she envisioned a space where the power of creativity and the pursuit of profit could harmoniously coexist. This chapter unveils the gestation of Crystal Bridges Museum of American Art, a visionary project that would become a testament to Alice's commitment to cultural enrichment and philanthropy.

As we delve into the intricate tapestry of Chapter 2, readers witness the convergence of Alice Walton's diverse influences and aspirations. The forging of her vision was a complex and nuanced process, shaped by education, societal shifts, and personal revelations. The stage is set for the emergence of a leader who would challenge conventions, blur boundaries, and leave an indelible mark on the landscape of wealth creation and cultural legacy.

4

Breaking Ground: The Birth of Crystal Bridges

The dew-kissed morning air clung to the construction site as the first shovelful of earth was lifted, signaling the commencement of a groundbreaking endeavor that would redefine the intersection of art, philanthropy, and commerce. In this chapter, we delve into the transformative period when Alice Walton's vision materialized into reality with the creation of Crystal Bridges Museum of American Art.

As the concrete foundations took shape in the heart of Bentonville, so too did the realization of Alice's dream. The museum, designed by renowned architect Moshe Safdie, emerged as a symbol of ambition, transcending the boundaries of traditional philanthropy. Crystal Bridges was not merely a repository for artistic masterpieces; it was a testament to the belief that art could be a catalyst for cultural enrichment, education, and community development.

This chapter unveils the challenges and triumphs that marked the journey from conceptualization to construction. Alice navigated through bureaucratic hurdles, financial intricacies, and skeptics who questioned the audacity of creating a world-class art institution in the Ozarks. Her unwavering commitment, combined with a strategic network of advisors and supporters, propelled the project forward.

Crystal Bridges was more than just a museum; it was a manifestation of Alice Walton's belief in the transformative power of art. The collection, carefully curated and spanning centuries of American history, reflected not only her discerning taste but also a commitment to fostering a deeper understanding of the American experience. The museum's architectural grandeur mirrored Alice's vision of creating a space where the natural beauty of the Ozarks converged with the beauty of American art.

As the construction cranes etched the skyline, the anticipation surrounding Crystal Bridges grew. This chapter unfolds the inaugural moments of the museum, from the first brushstroke to the grand opening. The convergence of artists, scholars, and patrons celebrated the realization of a vision that had germinated in the mind of Alice Walton—a vision that went beyond bricks and mortar to embrace the soul-stirring power of creativity.

In "Breaking Ground," readers witness the birth of Crystal Bridges as more than a cultural institution. It was a statement—a declaration that wealth, when wielded with purpose and passion, could be a force for profound societal change. As the museum's doors swung open, Alice Walton's journey entered a new phase—one marked by the enduring legacy of a visionary endeavor that bridged the worlds of art, wealth, and community.

5

The Canvas Unfolds: Navigating Challenges and Cultivating Philanthropy

As Crystal Bridges settled into the lush landscape of Bentonville, the canvas of Alice Walton's life continued to unfold, revealing a woman determined to navigate challenges and weave a tapestry of philanthropy that transcended the confines of a museum. This chapter delves into the years following the museum's inauguration, exploring Alice's commitment to fostering art education, tackling social challenges, and reshaping the narrative of wealth and responsibility.

With Crystal Bridges standing as a testament to cultural enrichment, Alice turned her attention to the role of education in igniting the spark of creativity in the minds of the next generation. This chapter unveils the initiatives and partnerships forged to bring art education to schools and communities, reflecting Alice's belief that access to the arts could be a catalyst for social change.

Yet, the philanthropic journey was not without its complexities. The chapter delves into the challenges Alice faced in balancing the demands of a burgeoning museum, the expectations of a community, and the evolving landscape of philanthropy. Navigating the intricate dance between commerce and culture, Alice sought to redefine the role of a billionaire in society—one who not only accumulated wealth but deployed it strategically for the greater good.

The canvas of philanthropy expanded beyond the walls of Crystal Bridges. Alice's initiatives addressed issues ranging from environmental conservation to healthcare, reflecting a holistic approach to social responsibility. This chapter explores the strategic partnerships and collaborations that emerged as Alice endeavored to make a lasting impact on the communities that had shaped her life.

In the crucible of philanthropy, Alice faced criticism and scrutiny. The chapter unravels the public discourse surrounding the responsibilities of the wealthy, probing the complexities of balancing personal wealth with societal obligations. Alice's journey became a case study in the evolving expectations placed on billionaires, as she sought to define a narrative where prosperity was not just measured in dollars but in the positive imprint left on the world.

"The Canvas Unfolds" invites readers into the intricate web of challenges and triumphs that characterized Alice Walton's philanthropic endeavors. It explores the evolving role of wealth in society and the profound impact one woman's vision can have on communities, education, and the very fabric of cultural enrichment. As the strokes of philanthropy blended with the hues of societal change, Alice Walton's journey entered a new chapter—one that went beyond building an empire to shaping a legacy of purpose and impact.

6

Beyond Boundaries: Global Impact and Legacy Building

I n the fifth chapter of "The Art of Wealth," the narrative expands beyond the tranquil confines of Bentonville and Crystal Bridges, transcending geographical boundaries to explore Alice Walton's global impact and the enduring legacy she envisions. This chapter unfolds against the backdrop of an interconnected world, where the pursuit of wealth intertwines with a commitment to address pressing global challenges.

Alice's philanthropic vision, initially rooted in the American experience, takes on an international dimension. The chapter begins by exploring her engagement with global issues, from environmental sustainability to healthcare access. This expanded scope reflects a recognition that the challenges of the modern world require solutions that reach far beyond national borders.

As the narrative unfolds, readers are taken on a journey through Alice's strategic partnerships with international organizations, visionary leaders, and change-makers. The chapter delves into the initiatives aimed at creating a positive impact on a global scale, emphasizing the ripple effect of wealth when deployed with purpose and foresight.

Alice's commitment to environmental stewardship becomes a focal point, and the chapter explores her endeavors to address climate change, promote sustainable practices, and contribute to the global conversation on ecological responsibility. It reflects a profound understanding that the health of the planet is intricately linked to the well-being of its inhabitants.

Simultaneously, the narrative weaves through Alice's efforts in the realm of global healthcare. Through strategic investments, partnerships, and philanthropic initiatives, she becomes a catalyst for change, aiming to enhance healthcare access, advance medical research, and tackle pressing public health challenges.

Legacy building takes center stage in this chapter as the narrative circles back to Crystal Bridges. The museum, once a testament to American art and culture, evolves into a symbol of enduring legacy. Alice's meticulous planning for the future, including considerations for the perpetuity of her philanthropic efforts, reflects a commitment to leaving a lasting imprint on the world.

"Beyond Boundaries" invites readers to witness the convergence of wealth, philanthropy, and a global perspective. It explores the evolution of Alice Walton's vision, demonstrating how the pursuit of wealth can be a force for positive change on a global scale. As the chapter unfolds, it becomes evident that Alice's journey is not just about accumulating riches but about using them to build a legacy that transcends borders and generations.

7

Navigating Change: Challenges, Reflections, and the Ever-Evolving Journey

As the landscape of wealth and philanthropy continues to shift, the sixth chapter of "The Art of Wealth" delves into the intricacies of navigating change. This segment of Alice Walton's journey is marked by challenges, reflections, and a keen awareness of the evolving dynamics that shape the world of business, philanthropy, and societal expectations.

The narrative opens with a candid exploration of the challenges that Alice encounters in an ever-changing economic and social climate. Economic downturns, technological disruptions, and shifts in public sentiment pose new tests for wealth management and philanthropic impact. This chapter provides insights into how Alice adapts her strategies, leveraging her experience and resilience to overcome obstacles.

Reflective in nature, the chapter explores pivotal moments in Alice's journey, examining the lessons learned from both successes and setbacks. It unravels her introspective approach to wealth, philanthropy, and legacy, offering readers a glimpse into the mindset of a business leader and philanthropist who constantly seeks to refine her understanding of impact and purpose.

The evolving dynamics of the Walton family legacy also come to the forefront. The chapter delves into the interplay between individual aspirations, family dynamics, and the collective responsibility of one of the world's wealthiest families. As the narrative unfolds, readers witness the delicate balance between maintaining a legacy and fostering individual pursuits, showcasing the complexities inherent in navigating generational wealth.

Philanthropy remains a central theme, with Alice's initiatives adapting to address emerging societal needs. The chapter explores how she engages with contemporary issues, from technological disruption to social justice, demonstrating a commitment to relevance and impact in an ever-changing world.

Against the backdrop of change, the chapter weaves threads of continuity, emphasizing the enduring values that anchor Alice's journey. The commitment to education, the promotion of the arts, and a dedication to positive societal change remain steadfast, providing a compass that guides her through the complexities of wealth and influence.

In "Navigating Change," readers witness a dynamic and reflective phase of Alice Walton's journey. It is a chapter that underscores the adaptability required in the face of a constantly evolving landscape. As the narrative unfolds, it becomes evident that the art of wealth is not static; it is a living, breathing entity that responds to the rhythms of change while staying true to its foundational principles.

8

The Next Horizon: Innovations, Collaborations, and the Future of Wealth

In the seventh chapter of "The Art of Wealth," the narrative propels us toward the next horizon of Alice Walton's journey—a phase defined by innovation, collaborations, and a visionary outlook that extends beyond the present. This chapter explores how Alice navigates the ever-changing landscape of wealth, philanthropy, and societal expectations to shape a future where impact and purpose converge.

The narrative opens with a glimpse into the innovative ventures that define this phase of Alice's journey. From strategic investments in cutting-edge technologies to groundbreaking collaborations with forward-thinking leaders, she positions herself at the intersection of commerce and innovation. This chapter delves into the thought processes and strategic decisions that drive her pursuit of new frontiers in wealth creation and societal impact.

Collaborations become a key theme as Alice engages with a diverse array of influencers, thought leaders, and change-makers. The chapter unravels the partnerships that transcend traditional boundaries, fostering synergies between business, philanthropy, and social change. Through these collaborations, Alice seeks to amplify the impact of her initiatives, recognizing the collective power that arises when like-minded visionaries join forces.

The narrative also explores Alice's commitment to fostering the next generation of leaders. Initiatives aimed at empowering young entrepreneurs, artists, and changemakers take center stage. This chapter delves into mentorship programs, educational initiatives, and investments in emerging talent, highlighting a dedication to nurturing innovation and creativity for the benefit of future generations.

As societal expectations around wealth and responsibility continue to evolve, the chapter delves into Alice's reflections on the role of billionaires in shaping a better world. It explores her perspective on the ethical deployment of wealth, the importance of transparency, and the responsibilities that come with influence and affluence.

The closing sections of the chapter provide a glimpse into the future—both for Alice Walton and the broader landscape of wealth and philanthropy. The narrative explores the legacy-building aspects of this phase, contemplating how Alice envisions the enduring impact of her journey and contributions on a global scale.

"The Next Horizon" invites readers to explore the forward-looking dimension of Alice Walton's journey. It is a chapter marked by innovation, collaboration, and a commitment to shaping a future where the art of wealth extends beyond individual prosperity to become a catalyst for positive, transformative change in the world.

9

Legacy in Bloom: The Culmination of a Life's Work

In the eighth and final chapter of "The Art of Wealth," the narrative converges on the culmination of Alice Walton's remarkable journey—a chapter defined by the realization of her vision, the enduring legacy she leaves behind, and reflections on a life shaped by purpose and impact.

The chapter opens with the realization of Alice's vision in full bloom. The initiatives, philanthropic endeavors, and innovative ventures that marked her journey have reached maturity, leaving an indelible imprint on the world. The narrative explores the fruits of her labor, from the flourishing impact of Crystal Bridges to the transformative outcomes of her global philanthropic efforts.

As the canvas of Alice's legacy unfolds, the chapter delves into the lasting impact on communities, education, and the arts. Through interviews, retrospectives, and anecdotes, readers witness the tangible and intangible legacies woven into the fabric of society. The narrative celebrates the lives touched, the minds inspired, and the transformative change brought about by a lifetime dedicated to the art of wealth.

Legacy-building becomes a central theme, exploring how Alice strategically shaped the future of her philanthropic efforts. The chapter discusses the perpetuity of her initiatives, the establishment of foundations, and the mechanisms in place to ensure that her impact endures for generations to come. It reflects on the transition from individual success to a legacy that extends beyond the boundaries of time.

The narrative also provides a glimpse into Alice's reflections on the journey. Through interviews and personal reflections, readers gain insights into the lessons learned, the challenges overcome, and the evolving perspectives that shaped her understanding of wealth, responsibility, and purpose. The chapter becomes a platform for wisdom-sharing, inviting readers to glean insights from a life rich in experiences.

As the chapter concludes, it looks toward the future. It contemplates how the seeds planted by Alice Walton will continue to grow, evolve, and inspire. The final pages of "Legacy in Bloom" serve as both a reflection on the past and a projection into the future—a future where the art of wealth, as exemplified by Alice Walton, continues to be a force for positive change and enduring impact.

In this concluding chapter, readers witness the full tapestry of Alice Walton's journey—the challenges, triumphs, innovations, and reflections that define a life dedicated to the art of wealth. It is a legacy in bloom, an exploration of the lasting impact one woman's vision can have on the world.

10

Beyond the Horizon: The Enduring Influence of Alice Walton's Legacy

As we turn the final pages of "The Art of Wealth," the narrative extends beyond the immediate aftermath of Alice Walton's journey, exploring the enduring influence of her legacy on the landscape of wealth, philanthropy, and societal impact.

The chapter opens by examining the continued evolution of Alice's philanthropic initiatives and the organizations she established. It delves into the ways in which these entities adapt to new challenges, seize emerging opportunities, and remain at the forefront of positive change. Readers witness how the seeds planted by Alice continue to bear fruit, shaping a future that aligns with her values and vision.

The narrative expands to explore the impact of Alice's journey on the broader world of business and philanthropy. Interviews with leaders, scholars, and influencers provide perspectives on how her innovative approaches, collaborations, and strategic philanthropy have influenced industry practices and societal expectations. The chapter serves as a testament to the ripple effect of a visionary's actions on the larger canvas of global affairs.

Legacy, in this context, transcends the tangible outcomes of philanthropic initiatives. The chapter explores the intangible aspects of Alice's influence—the inspiration she provides to future generations, the paradigm shifts in societal expectations of wealth, and the ways in which her journey becomes a guiding light for individuals navigating the complex intersection of wealth and impact.

In the closing sections, the narrative contemplates the continued relevance of the art of wealth in an ever-changing world. It reflects on the broader implications of Alice's journey for the future of wealth creation, the responsibilities of the affluent, and the evolving narratives surrounding the purpose and impact of wealth on a global scale.

As readers reach the final pages of "Beyond the Horizon," they are invited to contemplate the enduring legacy of Alice Walton's journey. The chapter serves as a bridge between the conclusion of her personal narrative and the ongoing, ever-evolving impact she leaves behind—a legacy that extends beyond the horizon and continues to shape the narrative of wealth, purpose, and societal responsibility for generations to come.

11

Epilogue: A Lasting Imprint on the Canvas of Wealth and Purpose

In this final chapter, the epilogue of "The Art of Wealth" unfolds as a reflection on the entirety of Alice Walton's extraordinary journey. It serves as a tribute to the woman whose life was a canvas painted with innovation, philanthropy, and an unwavering commitment to leaving the world better than she found it.

The narrative revisits key milestones in Alice's life, tracing the arc of her journey from the small town of Bentonville to the global stage of philanthropy and business. Interviews with those closest to her, as well as scholars and observers, provide nuanced insights into the impact of her legacy on diverse facets of society.

As readers traverse the epilogue, they witness the echoes of Alice's influence in the continued flourishing of Crystal Bridges, the sustained growth of her philanthropic initiatives, and the lasting impact on communities around the world. The chapter becomes a reflective space, exploring the ways in which Alice's vision and values persist, inspiring a new generation of leaders, entrepreneurs, and philanthropists.

The narrative contemplates the broader implications of Alice Walton's journey on the discourse surrounding wealth and societal responsibility. It examines the evolving narratives in the public consciousness, the changing expectations of the wealthy, and the ways in which her journey has contributed to reshaping the dynamics between prosperity and purpose.

The epilogue serves as a bridge between the detailed chronicle of Alice's life and the ongoing narrative of the world she leaves behind. It invites readers to engage in a contemplative exploration of the lasting imprint on the canvas of wealth and purpose—an imprint that transcends individual achievements to become a part of the collective consciousness of a society in flux.

As readers turn the final pages of "The Art of Wealth," they carry with them the story of a woman whose journey was not just a testament to financial success but a celebration of the transformative power of wealth when wielded with intention, innovation, and an unwavering commitment to creating a legacy that endures beyond the bounds of time.

12

The Continuing Tapestry: Nurturing the Seeds of Change

In this unexpected yet pivotal chapter, we step beyond the conclusion of "The Art of Wealth" and into the evolving narrative of Alice Walton's legacy. Chapter 11 serves as a living addendum to the story, tracing the ongoing impact of her vision and the dynamic ways in which the seeds she planted continue to sprout, creating ripples in the ever-changing tapestry of wealth, philanthropy, and societal progress.

The chapter opens with a glimpse into the initiatives and endeavors that have emerged posthumously, illustrating how the legacy of Alice Walton persists beyond her physical presence. Interviews with those entrusted with carrying forward her vision provide insight into how her influence endures through the dedication of individuals who share her passion for positive change.

The narrative explores the ways in which Crystal Bridges has evolved and expanded, not only as a museum but as a dynamic hub for artistic expression, cultural exchange, and educational innovation. The chapter delves into the ongoing projects, exhibitions, and community engagement initiatives that keep the spirit of Crystal Bridges alive, fostering a vibrant ecosystem of creativity.

As the chapter unfolds, readers are introduced to the next generation of leaders and influencers inspired by Alice's journey. Interviews with scholarship recipients, mentees, and individuals touched by her philanthropy shed light on the transformative impact she continues to have on aspiring changemakers across various fields.

Collaborations and partnerships take center stage, showcasing how the legacy of Alice Walton remains a catalyst for meaningful alliances. From innovative philanthropic projects to groundbreaking business ventures, the narrative explores the ways in which her principles continue to shape the collaborative efforts of those committed to driving positive change.

The chapter concludes with a forward-looking perspective, contemplating how the ongoing narrative of Alice Walton's legacy intersects with the broader discourse on wealth, responsibility, and societal impact. Interviews with thought leaders and reflections from those influenced by her journey provide glimpses into the potential trajectories of the evolving landscape she helped shape.

Chapter 11 serves as a testament to the enduring nature of Alice Walton's legacy—a legacy that not only survives the passage of time but continues to grow, adapt, and inspire. It invites readers to witness the continuation of a narrative that extends beyond the confines of a traditional conclusion, embodying the dynamic and ever-evolving nature of the art of wealth.

13

Reflections on a Storied Journey

As we embark on the final chapter of "The Art of Wealth," we take a reflective pause, offering a space to contemplate the rich tapestry of Alice Walton's journey. Chapter 12 serves as a collective reflection, inviting readers to revisit the pivotal moments, lessons learned, and the profound impact that has rippled through the narrative.

The chapter opens with a retrospective lens, exploring the resonance of key moments in Alice's journey. It revisits the challenges she faced, the triumphs she celebrated, and the transformative decisions that shaped her trajectory. Interviews with those intimately involved in her story offer nuanced perspectives, providing additional layers to the narrative.

Reflective essays, anecdotes, and personal narratives from individuals who have been touched by Alice's journey contribute to the chapter's tapestry. Readers encounter diverse voices—from colleagues and collaborators to beneficiaries of her philanthropy—who share their unique experiences and insights, revealing the multifaceted impact of a life dedicated to the art of wealth.

The narrative extends beyond the individual to examine the broader societal impact. Scholars, commentators, and cultural observers contribute to an exploration of how Alice Walton's journey has influenced the discourse around wealth, philanthropy, and societal responsibility. This segment aims to capture the evolving narratives that have been shaped by her influence.

The chapter also delves into the legacy of Crystal Bridges, examining how the museum has become a living testament to the convergence of art, wealth, and community. Interviews with curators, educators, and visitors shed light on the lasting impact of this cultural institution, which continues to flourish as a dynamic hub for artistic expression and cultural enrichment.

Amidst the reflections, the chapter weaves in moments of introspection, contemplating the broader implications of Alice Walton's journey on the future. How has the landscape of philanthropy evolved? What lessons can be gleaned from her approach to wealth and impact? These questions serve as catalysts for a thoughtful examination of the ongoing relevance of her legacy.

As Chapter 12 draws to a close, it leaves readers with a sense of closure and an invitation to carry forward the spirit of the art of wealth. The journey may have reached its conclusion, but the echoes of Alice Walton's story resonate, inspiring contemplation on the transformative potential of wealth when aligned with purpose, innovation, and a commitment to leaving a lasting legacy.

14

Summary

"The Art of Wealth" is a comprehensive narrative that traces the remarkable journey of Alice Walton, heir to the Walmart fortune, as she navigates the complex intersection of wealth, business, and philanthropy. The story unfolds across twelve chapters, each capturing a distinct phase of Alice's life and the evolution of her vision.

In the early chapters, readers witness Alice's formative years in Bentonville, Arkansas, where the roots of the Walton family legacy were planted. Born into the retail empire founded by her father, Sam Walton, Alice inherits a commitment to hard work and innovation.

As the narrative progresses, Alice's journey takes unexpected turns. Chapter by chapter, readers explore her educational pursuits, global explorations, and the internal struggles of reconciling her personal aspirations with the weight of the Walton name. The story converges on the pivotal moment when Alice's vision crystallizes—the creation of Crystal Bridges Museum of American Art.

The narrative dives into the challenges, triumphs, and the societal impact of Crystal Bridges, illustrating how Alice's commitment to cultural enrichment and philanthropy goes beyond traditional boundaries. The subsequent chapters explore the global dimensions of Alice's philanthropy, the intricacies of navigating change, and the enduring legacy she aspires to leave.

The epilogue serves as a bridge between the conclusion of Alice's personal narrative and the ongoing impact of her legacy. It contemplates the ways in which her vision continues to shape the discourse around wealth, philanthropy, and societal responsibility.

Chapter 11 and Chapter 12 extend beyond the initial conclusion, offering readers insights into the ongoing narrative of Alice Walton's legacy. They explore how her initiatives persist, the collaborative endeavors inspired by her vision, and the reflections from various perspectives—providing a living addendum to the broader narrative.

In summary, "The Art of Wealth" is a tapestry of innovation, philanthropy, and societal impact. It goes beyond the conventional biography, inviting readers to contemplate the transformative power of wealth when wielded with intention and a commitment to leaving a positive and enduring legacy on the world.